My New World

Georgina Conway

Text copyright © Georgina Conway 1998
Illustrations, Mike Carter
Cover design, David Andrassy
Back cover photograph, Stella Fitzpatrick
Editor, Stella Fitzpatrick

First published & distributed by Gatehouse Books Ltd in 1998
Reprinted 2000 by Gatehouse Books Ltd
Hulme Adult Education Centre, Stretford Road, Manchester M15 5FQ
Printed by RAP Ltd., Rochdale.
ISBN 0 906253 56 X
British Library cataloguing in publication data:
A catalogue record for this book is available from the British Library

Two Gatehouse Book Selection Groups recommended this story for publication.
Many thanks for their work to Nora Ashton, Irene Leech, Mary Morris and Josie
Roche at Newton House & Sandra Brown, Beverley Chadderton, Christine Jones,
Gail Rocca, John Smith, Kevin Summers & Hugh Walsh at Spurley Hey Centre

Thanks also to basic skills groups run by Manchester Adult Education Services at
The Birtles, Greenheys, Plant Hill and Varna Centres and to Moya Curran's group in
Stockport, with whom we piloted a first draft of this book

Gatehouse also acknowledges continued financial support from Manchester City
Council and North West Arts Board

Gatehouse is a member of the Federation of Worker Writers & Community
Publishers

Introduction

Hello. My name is Georgina Conway.
I am twenty six years old and I live in Manchester.
I have three beautiful children.

I decided to write this story to help you understand
what bullying can do to a person.
I would also like to say, if you feel the same as I did,
do not put up with it. Tell someone.
Things will not get worse.
Someone can help you
and stop all the pain that you are going through.

Georgina Conway

I would like to thank my partner and all my family
for their support, and also my tutor.

From what I can remember,
I did not like school very much.
In fact, I hated it.
I was bullied from when I was little
until the day I left.

I would cry myself to sleep
every Sunday night,
knowing I had to go to school
for the next week and get bullied.
I hated every day of it.

The worst thing
that can happen to a child,
is being bullied.
You feel so lonely
and have no confidence in yourself.
I also found it hard to do the work.
I just could not concentrate.

I remember going to see
a special teacher
who worked with children
who had learning problems.

The other children would pick on me
over that,
saying I was thick
and should be in a special school
for thick kids.

Then my problems
started getting worse.
I did not want to go to school.
I would always lie to my mum,
hoping she would let me stay off.

But even that only worked for a while,
because when I was really sick,
my mum did not believe me
and I got sent to school.
I will always remember
my mum saying
I was like the boy who cried wolf*.

*See page 27

I was a quiet child at school
and had no friends.
It was like I was digging a hole.
I just kept getting deeper and deeper
into trouble.
Firstly, I had no friends,
then I got bullied,
then I could not concentrate
on my work
and then I did not want
to go to school.

None of the teachers liked me.
Well, I do not know
whether they liked me or not,
or if they had just given up
trying to help me.

The bullying was the one thing
most damaging in my later life.
I have never had confidence.
I used to hate myself
and always wanted
to be someone else.

I would always put myself down
and I still do.
It is hard to get out of the habit.
When you have been told
that you are thick
for most of your life,
you start to believe it.

I got the confidence
to go back to night school
for my children,
to help them with their homework.
I think that the extra help
that they get at home
is very important.

My daughter is seven
and she needs lots of help.
Every night she has homework
and I am so pleased
that I can sit down and work with her.
But I never thought
that I would get as far
as being able to help my children.

At night school
everyone has come back
for the same reasons
although they are all
at different levels.

The tutors are great too.
I went through stages where I thought
it was a waste of time,
that I was never going to learn anything
and that I was getting nowhere.

I had no confidence
and when I wrote stories or letters
I would not like anyone
to look at them.
But it is the confidence
that the tutors have in you
and your work
that keeps you going back.

I also think that you have
to have willpower
to stick at it and ask yourself,
what have I got to lose?

I have been going to night school
for a year now
and it has helped me
to get some confidence.
This confidence
has made a big difference in my life.

If I am not happy about something now
I will not let people tell me what to do
and boss me around.
I will complain about it
either by letter
or just telling them, face to face.

It has not just given me

the confidence

to stand up for myself and my children

but it has made me feel really good.

My parents and family

are so proud of me.

Going to night school

has been great for me.

I will be getting a certificate
for Wordpower* level 1
and I will go on to level 2,
then on to college.
I have not yet decided
what I want to do
but I am very interested
in helping children.
I think I am a good person
to help children deal with being bullied,
because I have been bullied myself.

* Wordpower is a basic skills course

I am now thinking of the future.

So you can see,

that going to night school

has been the best thing

I have ever done.

The Boy Who Cried "Wolf!" (See p11)

In this story, a boy looks after a flock of sheep. When he is bored, he shouts, "Wolf!" People come to chase away the wolf. But there is no wolf.

One day, a wolf really does attack the sheep. When the boy cries "Wolf!" no one believes him. Some of his sheep are killed.

Gatehouse Books

Gatehouse is a unique publisher

Our writers are adults who are developing their basic reading and writing skills. Their ideas and experiences make fascinating material for any reader, but are particularly relevant for adults working on their reading and writing skills. The writing strikes a chord - a shared experience of struggling against many odds.

The format of our books is clear and uncluttered. The language is familiar and the text is often line-broken, so that each line ends at a natural pause.

Gatehouse books are both popular and respected within Adult Basic Education throughout the English speaking world. They are also a valuable resource within secondary schools, Social Services and within the Prison Education Service and Probation Services.

Booklist available

Gatehouse Books
Hulme Adult Education Centre
Stretford Road
Manchester
M15 5FQ
Tel/Fax: 0161 226 7152
E-mail: office@gatehousebooks.org.uk
Website: www.gatehousebooks.org.uk

The Gatehouse Publishing Charity Ltd is a registered charity, no. 1011042
Gatehouse Books Ltd is a company limited by guarantee, reg no. 2619614